HOW MUCH IS It?

Adam Schaefer

Rourke

Publishing LLC
Vero Beach, Florida 32964

www.rourkepublishing.com

PHOTO CREDITS: © James Bowers: cover; © Jim Jurica: title page; © Tari Faris: page 13; © foxygrl: page 21; © Renee Brady: page 22

Editor: Robert Stengard-Olliges

Cover design by Nicola Stratford.

Library of Congress Cataloging-in-Publication Data

Schaefer, Adam.
  How much is it? : a book about counting coins / Adam Schaefer.
     p. cm. -- (My first math)
  Includes index.
  ISBN 1-59515-973-8 (hardcover)
  ISBN 1-59515-949-5 (paperback)
  1. Counting--Juvenile literature. 2. Coins,
American--Mathematics--Juvenile literature. I. Title.
  QA113.S376 2007
  513.2'11--dc22
                            2006019780

Printed in the USA

CG/CG

Rourke Publishing

www.rourkepublishing.com – sales@rourkepublishing.com
Post Office Box 3328, Vero Beach, FL 32964

Table of Contents

Pennies

A **penny** is a U.S. **coin**. It is **money**. You can use money to buy something.

1 Penny = 1 Cent

What can you buy with a penny? Not much! But five pennies equal a **nickel**.

Five Cents

A nickel is a U.S. coin. What can you buy with a nickel? Not much! It is worth only five cents. It is equal to five pennies.

1 Nickle = 5 Cents

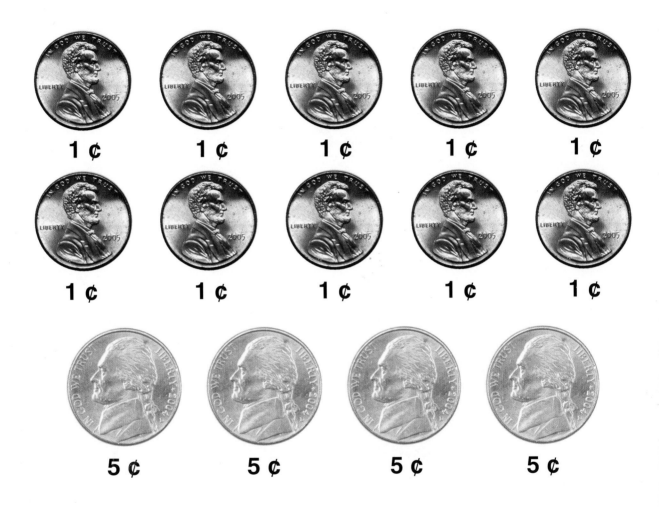

1 ¢ 1 ¢ 1 ¢ 1 ¢ 1 ¢

1 ¢ 1 ¢ 1 ¢ 1 ¢ 1 ¢

5 ¢ 5 ¢ 5 ¢ 5 ¢

You can add pennies and nickels to buy something. If you add ten pennies and four nickels, how much is that?

Ten Cents

A **dime** is a U.S. coin. It is worth ten cents. That means it is equal to ten pennies or two nickels.

1 Dime = 10 Cents

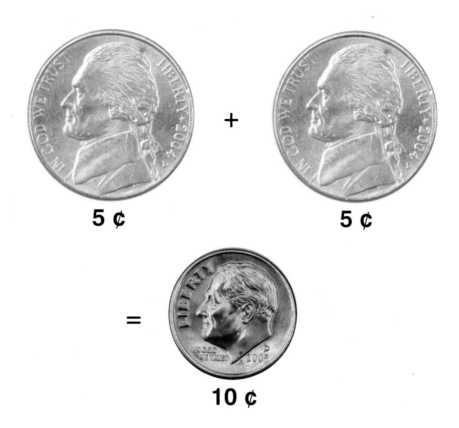

5 ¢ + 5 ¢

= 10 ¢

What can you buy for ten cents? Not much! But you can add your dimes to your nickels and pennies. If you add ten pennies, one nickel, and one dime, how much do you have?

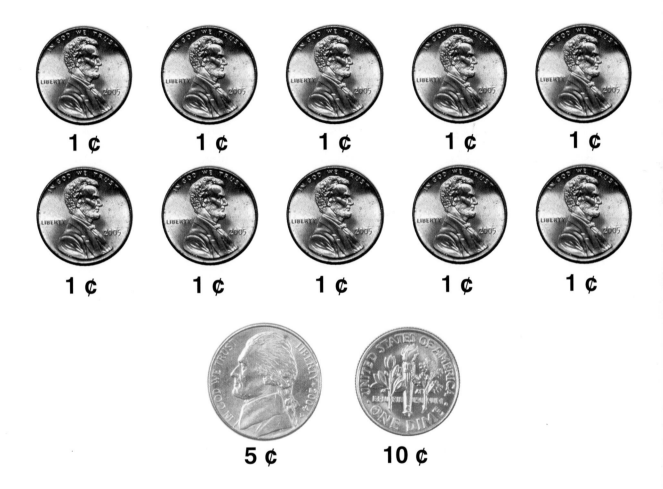

1 ¢ 1 ¢ 1 ¢ 1 ¢ 1 ¢

1 ¢ 1 ¢ 1 ¢ 1 ¢ 1 ¢

5 ¢ 10 ¢

What can you do with pennies, nickels, and dimes? You can save them in a piggy bank. You can use them in parking meters. You can make a wish in a fountain.

You can add them together to make enough to buy something. If you add three dimes, three nickels, and three pennies together, how much money is that?

10 ¢   10 ¢   10 ¢

5 ¢   5 ¢   5 ¢

1 ¢   1 ¢   1 ¢

Twenty-five Cents

A **quarter** is a U.S. coin. It is worth 25 cents. Twenty-five cents can be made with pennies, nickels, and dimes.

1 Quarter = 25 Cents

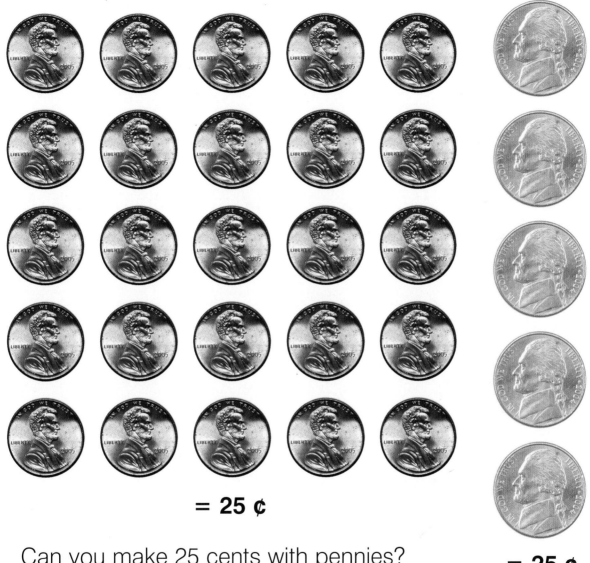

= 25 ¢

Can you make 25 cents with pennies?
Can you make 25 cents with nickels?

= 25 ¢

Can you make 25 cents with dimes? Count each dime —10, 20, 30….too much! Count again, 10, 20,…. You need five cents more. You can use five pennies or a nickel. Now you have 25 cents.

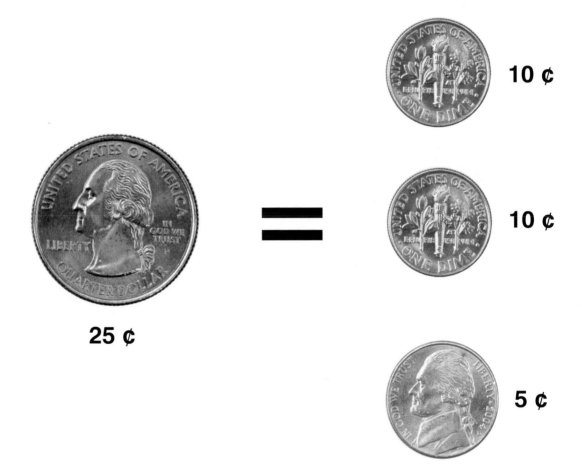

25 ¢

10 ¢

10 ¢

5 ¢

A Dollar

A **dollar** is U.S. money. It is worth 100 cents. If you have 100 pennies, you can change them for a dollar. If you have 10 dimes, you can change them for a dollar. How many nickels do you need to change them to a dollar?

$1.00 = 100 Cents

Every time you buy something, you can use pennies, nickels, dimes, quarters, or dollars. They are all U.S. money.

Glossary

coin (KOIN) — a small piece of metal used for money

dime (DIME) — US coin worth ten cents

dollar (DOL ur) — US paper money worth 100 cents

money (MUHN ee) — coins and paper bills used to buy goods and services in a country

nickel (NIK uhl) — US coin worth five cents

penny (PEN ee) — US coin worth one cent

quarter (KWOR tur) — US coin worth 25 cents

Index

Further Reading

Cooper, Jason. *American Bills and Coins.* Rourke Publishing, 2004.
Snodgrass, Mary Ellen. *Coins and Currency : a Historical Encyclopedia.* McFarland & Co., 2003.
Williams, Rozanne Lanczak. *Learning About Coins.* Gareth Stevens, 2004.

Websites To Visit

www.usmint.gov/kids
www.moneyfactory.gov/kids/start.html
www.ssa.gov/kids/kids.htm

About The Author

A.R. Schaefer has written more than 40 books for children. He lives in Chapel Hill, N.C.